The Local Historian at Work 5
General Editor: David

NEWSPAPERS
AND LOCAL HISTORY

Michael Murphy

Published by PHILLIMORE for
BRITISH ASSOCIATION FOR LOCAL HISTORY

1991

Published for
BRITISH ASSOCIATION FOR LOCAL HISTORY
by PHILLIMORE & CO. LTD.
Shopwyke Hall, Chichester, Sussex

ISBN 0 85033 782 8

Printed by Chichester Press Limited

CONTENTS

ACKNOWLEDGEMENTS

In preparing this book we have received valuable advice and practical assistance from the following individuals: Ian Coulson, Ruth Gordon, Huw Owen, David Pam, Michael Petty, Kate Thompson, Elizabeth Watthews.

For help with illustrations we are indebted to the Cambridgeshire Collection, the Kent History Centre, the Kent Messenger Group, the Leicestershire Collection, and the Suffolk Record Office.

The Cambridge Chronicle, 5 December 1913, p. 8.

THE HISTORY OF NEWSPAPERS

'Few things are sought with more eagerness, few things are sooner cast aside as worthless than a newspaper.' As far as most of the general public is concerned, these sentiments expressed during the reign of Queen Victoria still apply. As Professor Donald Read has emphasised, until recently even historians were slow to treat newspapers seriously as organs of public opinion.[1] They have always been used as quarries of factual evidence, either for national or for local history, but only *The Times* was regarded as important enough to merit attention in its own right.

Since the 1960s, however, local historians have developed important new approaches and the content of the subject has changed dramatically. One consequence is that the study of newspapers, and of the attitudes and opinions which they contain, has taken on a new breadth and sophistication. As a result we now have some fine examples of how local newspapers can enrich our understanding of the past. Temple Patterson in his political history of *Radical Leicester* (Leicester, 1956) has given us a first-class example of what can be done. His work was largely based on the detailed examination of four sets of local newspapers. Two other admirable examples are R. Newton's *Victorian Exeter* (Leicester, 1968) and Donald Read's *Press and People: Opinion in Three English Cities* (London, 1961).

The history of newspapers in England can be said to have begun around 1513 when a news pamphlet gave an eye-witness account of the Battle of Flodden. It has lists of casualties and was illustrated with a woodcut.[2] Nothing similar was to follow for almost a hundred years, until the emergence of English *Newsbooks* which appeared in London in the 1620s and were given an immense boost in the 1640s by the Civil War. In the 17th and early 18th centuries governments attempted to control newspapers by means of the Stamp Act; this certainly hampered them, but failed to prevent their growth. Provincial papers started with the *Norwich Post* in 1701 and *Bristol Post Boy* in 1702. Although most early newspapers are southern, the expanding north began to catch up after 1750. Williamson's *Liverpool Advertiser* was first published in 1756. But even in 1800 England could only boast 100 provincial newspapers, and generally speaking their readership and impact were not great. As Jeremy Black has stated, the 18th century was 'neither an age of mass politics nor of mass culture and the developments that hinted in those directions were limited'.[3]

The first half of the 19th century witnessed several important developments. The government, fearful of revolution, tried to curtail the press by increasing the stamp duty, until in 1815 it reached its highest point at 4d. per newspaper (equivalent today to about £2). These infamous 'taxes on knowledge' merely gave rise to an 'unstamped press' which in its outpourings mercilessly attacked the established order in Church and State. During this period editorials became a feature of even the provincial newspapers, which despite the duties continued to grow in size largely as a result of increasing literacy, improved printing technology, the growth of railways and the electric telegraph.

In 1855 the 'taxes on knowledge' were repealed, and this further stimulated the growth of the popular press. The second half of Victoria's reign saw an impressive flowering of provincial dailies, many now priced at 1d. a copy. Newspapers such as the *Manchester Guardian* combined detailed reporting of local news with lengthy and sophisticated comment on national events. Politics became the main ingredient, newspapers often being strongly partisan and in the provinces overwhelmingly Liberal in their affiliation. In larger towns where Liberals and Tories struggled for control, politicians were quick to exploit the unshackling of the press. Gladstone, Disraeli, Salisbury, Chamberlain and Lloyd George all made use of this new platform in order to further their own policies and ambitions. As agents and accomplices of these political leaders, newspaper owners and editors were rewarded with financial subsidies and confidential information, and in some cases they even received titles.[4]

In 1896 the establishment of the *Daily Mail* initiated another revolution. This daily newspaper won a mass circulation, and together with Sunday newspapers fuelled a brash and vulgar 'new journalism' which aimed to inform and to entertain. In the next few decades the modern national press took shape: on the one hand a small number of quality papers, dedicated to serious reporting and comment on the political, economic and cultural worlds; and on the other a number of cheaper, popular newspapers such as *The Mirror*, *Herald* and *Mail* which deliberately blended news and entertainment.[5] Total annual circulation went up from three million copies in 1918 to 117 million by 1958, as the great dailies led by 'press barons' such as Rothermere and Beaverbrook waged bitter circulation wars to win over the reading public. In the face of this growing metropolitan dominance the provincial press, by the 1960s, began to decline. Some local newspapers became weeklies again, others began to publish evening editions only. Most now returned to local news, sport and amusements, and left the reporting of national and international news to the major London dailies.[6]

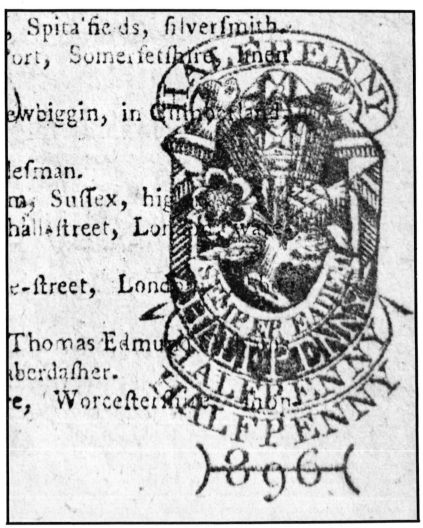

1. Stamp for duty of one-halfpenny on *Leicester Journal*, 27 June 1794, p.1.

6

NEWSPAPERS AS HISTORICAL SOURCES

'What is a newspaper?', asked a poem in the *Newcastle Courant* in 1876, 'and what does it contain?'

> News from all countries, and climes, my boy.
> Advertisements, essays, and rhymes, my boy.
> Mixed up with all sorts
> Of flying reports
> And published at regular times, my boy.
>
> Statistics, reflections, reviews, my boy.
> Little scraps to instruct and amuse, my boy.
> And lengthy debates
> Upon matters of State
> For wise-headed folks to peruse, my boy.[7]

The examples given in the verse are certainly not exhaustive, for newspapers can reveal a truly astonishing range of information and writing. No doubt there were always people who realised the retrospective or historical value of newspapers, as opposed to their immediate or contemporary use which is highly ephemeral. It is only in modern times, however, that this has constituted a major demand to see the files of back issues. In particular the growth of local and social history since the Second World War has enormously stimulated the historical use of local newspapers. When the chief preoccupations of historians were Acts of Parliament, division lists from the House of Commons and foreign diplomacy, the local press was of limited value. Today it is a different matter when, for example, professional and amateur historians want to know how cruel the Victorian Poor Law was, or how and

RIOT AT THE UNION WORKHOUSE. — A somewhat serious fracas occurred at the Workhouse on Tuesday morning. The scene of the disturbance was the young men's bed room (No. 9), occupied principally by youths under 20 years of age. It was commenced before daylight by some one flinging a utensil the whole length of the room. This gave occasion to a general *melée*, in which every pane of glass in the windows was smashed. After breakfast the more riotous of the party proceeded to smash the windows in the day room, in which they were. It was found impossible, as the smashing in the bed room was all over before daylight, to identify the guilty parties, but eight of those who were engaged in the latter offence were given in custody, and on being taken before the magistrates on Wednesday, two were dismissed for want of satisfactory evidence, four sentenced to 21 days, and two to three months' hard labour. The number of panes of glass broken is about 500, and the value £7. or £8.

2. Report of a riot among the young male inmates of a Union workhouse: *Leicester Journal*, 18 January 1856, p.3.

why leisure patterns changed during the 18th century. In tackling questions such as these the newspaper, arguably, is the most valuable single historical source in existence. As Francis Williams has stated: 'Newspapers are unique barometers of their age. They indicate more plainly than anything else the climate of the societies to which they belong'.[8]

Newspapers do vary, however, and they are not always of equal value to the historian. In the early 18th century provincial papers were local newsheets in name only. Most of their information was lifted from the major London dailies. For example, on 13 April 1723 the only items of local news in the *Newcastle Weekly Mercury* were 'the price of butter and the departure of ships'.[9] Consequently the researcher who hopes to find information on local elections, dissenting religion, poverty or conditions in workhouses will generally be disappointed. At that time printers (for that essentially is what they were) wanted not controversy but sales. As the *Northampton Mercury* put it (23 January 1721), 'publick reflections may bring an Odium upon the Paper, the Business of which is to amuse rather than reform'. They wanted their newspapers to be bought by Whig and Tory alike, and did not wish to provoke the launching of opposing prints. Expressions of local opinion, either in editorials or in letters to the press, were few and far between until very late in the century. Reporters were also a rarity (seen usually as either hacks or in the pay of officials) and local urban corporations were normally reluctant to provide minutes of their meetings.

While most 18th-century provincial newspapers are disappointingly limited for studying local political controversy and social change, they do provide unwitting testimony which has much to offer the assiduous local researcher. For example, valuable evidence can be dug out of advertisements, obituaries, enclosure notices, market prices and 'situations vacant'. Among other aspects of life regularly featuring are quack medicines, theatre billings, farm auctions, bankruptcies and election addresses. Except for correspondence and diaries, no better source exists for leisure activities such as horse-racing, fairs, cricket, boxing and the stage. This is only a sample of the wide range of historical enquiries which can be supported by systematic study of the earlier local newspapers.

By the early 19th century major changes had occurred. The onset of industrialisation, accompanied by the rise of a new and dynamic entrepreneurial class in the provinces, was to have profound and far-reaching effects on printing technology and the content of newspapers. More immediately, the war with France from 1793 to 1815 placed an unprecedented emphasis on newspapers as organs of public opinion and information. Whereas in the 18th century hardly any provincial printer would have hazarded an original article or editorial on public affairs, this was not the case after 1790. Under the stimulus of the French Revolution, printers became editors, the editorial column became one of the main propagators of political news and ideas, and the press was generally keener to play an active role in public life. At this stage we begin to see truly local newspapers voicing local views.

One of the most important pioneers in the transformation of the provincial press emerged, rather surprisingly, from the county and university town of Cambridge. From 1793 to 1803 Benjamin Flower, a radical Unitarian, published the *Cambridge Intelligencer*. From the outset, by using the editorial, he sought to instruct public opinion on the major issues of his day — the war, the reform of parliament and local government, religion and national politics. In doing this Flower showed that he had outgrown the 'scissors and paste' tradition and the earlier dependence on London newspapers. At the same time Joseph Gales of the *Sheffield Register* (1787-94) began using similar, if less extreme, editorials in the cause of reform.[10]

These early radical papers were ahead of their time, but by 1820 most of the big provincial centres were producing weekly prints such as the *Manchester Guardian*, *Newcastle Chronicle* and *Leeds Mercury*. The sales of these middle-class journals ranged from 2,000 to 5,000 copies a week. When after 1815 the government increased stamp duty in an effort to control the press, it merely encouraged the proliferation of a more radical 'unstamped press', and probably contributed to the enormous popularity of the best known radical newspaper of the day — the Chartist *Northern Star* — which regularly outsold all other provincial newspapers. It achieved the remarkable maximum circulation of about thirty thousand copies a week. However, serious politics alone were not enough to make a newspaper sell.

Confronted with falling sales in the 1830s, the radical editor Henry Hetherington promised that his *Twopenny Dispatch* would abound in 'Police Intelligence, in Murders, Rapes, Suicides, Burnings, Maimings, Theatricals, Races, Pugilism and . . . every sort of devilment that will make it sell'.[11] The abolition of the stamp duty in 1855 enabled the provincial press to flower in the final decades of the 19th century.

These changes, developments and opportunities meant that 19th-century newspapers could offer readers a more comprehensive and well-informed coverage of local and national events than their 18th-century predecessors. These changes also make them a more valuable source for local research today. Political historians can now read the editorial comment, peruse electoral addresses and letters to the press, scan local council reports and read in detail of the cut-and-thrust of local and national debate. Social historians can examine the rise of popular movements from Chartism to Temperance, and recreational activities from cricket to the music hall. Economic historians can chart the rise and fall of prices and

DISEWORTH INCLOSURE.

WE the COMMISSIONERS, appointed by "An Act for dividing and inclosing the open Fields, Meadows, Common Pastures, and Common Grounds, within the Lordship or Liberty of Diseworth, in the County of Leicester,"

DO HEREBY GIVE NOTICE,

To the Proprietors and Leaseholders of such Lands, Grounds, and Commons, that they do by themselves or their Agents, deliver in, in Writing, under his, her, or their Hands, to us, on Monday the 9th Day of June next, at the House of JOHN RAGG, known by the Sign of the Bull's Head, in Diseworth aforesaid, a Particular of all their several Claims in and over the said Lands to be inclosed, distinguishing the Number of Yard Lands and Parts of a Yard Land, with the specific Number of Horse, Cow, and Sheep Commons, and whether belonging to such Yard Lands or to any Messuages, Cottages, or other Right or Property whatsoever, and whether Tythe Free, or Tythable, Freehold, or Leasehold, or of what other Tenure they may be. Given under our Hands the 8th Day of May, 1794.

E. DAWSON,
SAM. WYATT,
WM. BURDETT.

3. Notice of a meeting convened by enclosure commissioners at Diseworth, Leicestershire: *Leicester Journal*, 16 May 1794, p.1.

wages, railways and migration, trade unions and family businesses. Welfare historians can read about workhouses and prisons, asylums and hospitals. All will be impressed by the ability of the local newspaper to shape the minds and move the consciences of the Victorian middle-class

Additionally the newspaper report can amplify and explain the concise and formal record. The minutes of a borough council or local railway company can sometimes be exasperatingly uninformative. Journalistic reporting on the other hand can put flesh on the bones of local controversy and add much needed detail to our understanding of local meetings. Interruptions and comments from the floor are usually documented, and generally speaking these newspaper reports are much more helpful to the researcher than the more anodyne formal minutes recorded by every kind of meeting from county council to local school board.

We have still not exhausted the historical potential of newspapers. News of property deals, especially the notices of sale and lease, can supplement title deeds and land-tax lists. Advertisements often mention acreages, field-names, values, occupiers' names, lost place-names, details of furnishings and so on. Quarter sessions and criminal trials were reported at length. Industrial, agricultural and trading information figures prominently — from cotton prices at Liverpool to corn prices at Ipswich or tobacco prices at Bristol.

Historians, biographers and genealogists frequently use newspapers to investigate the lives of individuals. They can begin with news of births and marriages — sometimes reported in much detail — and end with obituaries and often circumstances of death. Birth notices usually name the father and sometimes the mother and child also. They may note the father's job and the family address. Marriage entries are more standard but always mention out-of-county brides or grooms. Death notices in the 18th century are short, but tend to blossom in the Victorian era and can be very useful for filling in much-needed biographical detail.

Nor must we forget feature articles. One expects newspapers to contain news, but feature articles can be a most unexpected bonus. Many lie there to be discovered — the opening of a local railway station, a visit to a town workhouse or factory. In 1895, for example, reporters from the *Cambridge Independent Press* toured Cambridgeshire discussing with chairmen of newly formed parish councils the problems which they saw confronting their villages.

This is how Jack Ravensdale summed up the value of the *Cornish Times* in the late 19th century:

> Week by week it printed tabulated changes in mineral prices and mining shares, and international intelligence on minerals. This was the period of dramatic collapses in copper and tin, and the rise of china clay. It was the age of Great Depression in Cornish agriculture and mining (whether or not historians will allow such for the rest of the country and the rest of industry). The little weekly paper was also in effect a local *Economist*. The background of the diaspora of Cornish miners was never absent, and the advertisement columns were much occupied with emigrant ships offering passages to wherever there was metal ore in rock. Letters home, some of which may have been imaginary, were inserted as further advertisement for new worlds. But the news of the strikes in the coalfields that the Cornish miners had gone to break unwittingly, were conscientiously reported, as were the strikes by the Cornishmen when they found out how they had been used.[12]

Though we are only concerned with actual newspapers and news-sheets which gave 'hard news', it is worth drawing the attention of local historians to the many other 'papers' which can contribute towards our understanding of the past. These include trade papers such as the weekly *Railway Times*, various shipping gazettes, a large variety of sporting specials and temperance advocates, religious publications like the *Jewish Weekly*, *Catholic Monthly* and so on. Many of these curios or more specialised publications are listed in local gazetteers and directories.

Illustrations are another important characteristic of newspapers which can be of considerable historical value. Some local newspapers were capable of producing line drawings by the 1830s and 1840s. In the 1850s and 1860s a few provincial papers included the word 'illustrated' in their titles (for example *The Bridport Illustrated News*), but many lasted for only a few years and did not generally appear to be very popular. It was not until the 1880s

4. Mast-head of an early 18th-century newspaper with bird's-eye view of the town: *Ipswich Gazette*, 19-26 April 1735.

5. An illustration of an early railway-train with locomotive, tender and two coaches: *Cambridge Advertiser*, 17 June 1846.

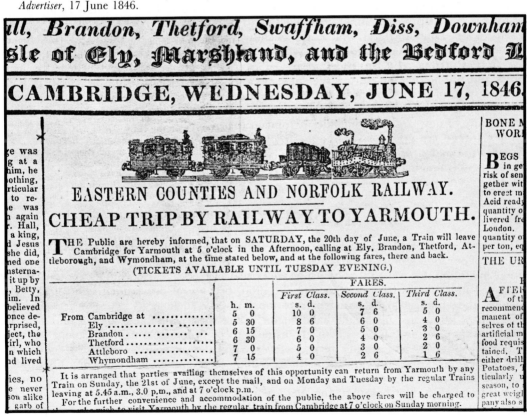

11

that illustrations and photographs became common, and they did not come into general use until after the First World War. One value of illustrations and drawings (especially in advertisements) is that they can throw light on more than one aspect of life. For example, street scenes can show names of shops, architectural changes, posters and other ephemera. After 1918 a principal feature of many local newspapers was to reproduce old photographs and illustrations sent in by readers weekly. These range (in the case of the *Cambridge Chronicle*) from general views of town streets and buildings to quite rare pictures — such as steam tugs working on the River Cam. Cartoons and photographs in the local press are particularly interesting in the period between the two World Wars.

As John West argues, no source of local history is as evocative of the atmosphere of a 19th-century town as its local newspaper. There is certainly no contemporary document more redolent of local identity and municipal pride. The pages of these proud local prints give an excellent insight into the Victorian period — recording many facets of town life, from the political aspirations of the town fathers through the varied economic and social demands of the new urban middle-class to the concerns and aspirations of the respectable skilled artisan. West found that of 375 municipal and county boroughs, only six have no recorded newspaper. For the remainder the average is about five per town, with Liverpool producing a grand total of 146 before 1920.[13] A notable example of urban history which draws heavily on the local press is the *History of Birmingham*, vol. 2, by Asa Briggs (1952).

Finally, several historians have concerned themselves with the press not simply as a resource for local and national history, but as a subject worthy of study in its own right. In his *Party Ideology and Popular Politics at the Accession of George III* (Cambridge, 1976), John Brewer showed how politicians in the 1760s used the press to help form public opinion. Arthur Aspinall charted the relationship between government, opposition and press in the period before the 'emancipation' of newspapers in his *Politics and the Press, c.1780-1850* (London, 1949). The story was taken further by Alan Lee in *The Origins of the Popular Press in England, 1855-1914* (London, 1976) and by Stephen Koss in the two volumes of *The Rise and Fall of the Political Press in Britain* (London, 1981-4). One of the most outstanding studies of the provincial press remains Donald Read's *Press and People, 1790-1850: Opinion in Three English Cities* (London, 1961), which explores how editors in Leeds, Sheffield and Manchester influenced the growth of middle-class reform movements. In my own *Cambridge Newspapers and Opinion, 1780-1850* (Cambridge, 1977), I examined the interaction between the local press and public opinion during the same period. Studies of individual newspapers have frequently been written by professional journalists whose concern is mainly with working conditions and the technicalities of production. While some are largely anecdotal, others are worthy of note and are generally helpful to the historian: for example, the magisterial *History of The Times* (5 vols., London, 1935-52); David Ayerst's *Guardian: Biography of a Newspaper* (London, 1971); and H. R. G. Whates' *The Birmingham Post, 1857-1957: a Centenary Retrospect* (Birmingham, 1957).

FINDING NEWSPAPERS

Until the 1960s files of local newspapers represented one of the largest sources of information in most of our local studies libraries, and yet one of the least accessible. Until the widespread use of microfilm this was probably just as well because excessive use would have irreparably damaged most stocks by now. Since about 1960, because of blossoming interest in social history, the enthusiasm of evangelists of local history such as W. G. Hoskins and the foresight of librarians, historians have begun to use these valuable 'runs' of national and local newspapers more fully. These are usually to be found in central reference libraries and those libraries and county record offices which house county historical collections. Many local libraries still possess their own files of originals, or they offer microfilms, though most have imperfect runs. York City Library, for example, has the *York Courant* dating from 1715, Northampton the *Mercury* from 1720, Gloucester the *Journal* from 1722 and Swansea the *Cambrian* from 1818. Some libraries have short runs of newspapers not recorded in the British Library Catalogue, for example Halifax Public Library has the *Journal*, 1801-11, and Hull the *Courant*, 1796-9. For more details of what libraries hold, the researcher can consult various regional surveys such as *Yorkshire Newspapers*, edited by G. E. Laughton and L. R. Stephen (l960); *The Newspapers of Northumberland and Durham*, by M. Milne (1971); and *Devon Newspapers*, by L. Smith (1973).

In order to make the most profitable use of surviving newspapers, the local historian must become acquainted with a number of finding aids. First, one should consult *The Times Tercentenary Handlist of English and Welsh Newspapers, 1620-1919* (1920), which lists when newspapers were founded, merged and ended. There are also two annual press guides which are to be found in almost every major reference library. These are *Willing's Press Guide* and *Benn's Press Directory*. They list, alphabetically, each town's current newspapers giving year of foundation and earlier titles. *The Newspaper Press Directory*, issued every year since 1846, will give the district in which each newspaper circulated. A useful guide to the 17th century is *A Census of Newspapers and Periodicals, 1620-1800*, by R. S. Crane, F. B. Kaye and M. E. Prior (1927), while the 18th century is well covered by *A Handlist of English Provincial Newspapers and Periodicals, 1700-1760*, by G. A. Cranfield (1952).

Welcome additions to this list are provided by the new *Bibliography of British Newspapers*. In the last two decades several volumes have already been published for individual counties, for example Wiltshire (1975), Durham and Northumberland (1972), Kent (1982), and Nottingham and Derbyshire (1987). Worth mentioning for those with an interest in the radical press of the 1830s is *A Descriptive Finding List of Unstamped British Periodicals, 1830-36*, by J. Weiner (l970). Though not complete, a most useful finding aid for all those embarking on research has been published recently by the Federation of Family History Societies: *Local Newspapers, 1750-1920: A Select Location List for England and Wales* by J. S. W. Gibson (1987, repr. 1989). Included in its coverage are the Channel Islands and the Isle of Man. Worth consulting also is *Family History from Newspapers* by E. McLoughlin (1986).

Two recent developments deserve special mention. Firstly, Harvester's programme for publishing 18th-century newspapers in microform has made a promising start with a fine composite film of the *Ipswich Journal*, 1729-65. Other work is in progress. The second development is Newsplan. This is a national scheme to record the local newspaper holdings of all English newspaper libraries and offices. It aims to list newspapers by title, giving locations and commenting on the quality of files. *Newsplan: Report for the South West* by Rosemary Wells (1986), the *East Midlands* by Ruth Gordon (1989), and the *Northern Region* by David Parry (1989), have already been published by the British Library. Volumes are being prepared for Yorkshire and Humberside, the West Midlands, the North West, Ireland and Wales.

Researchers who wish to examine newspaper files not available locally must go to the National Newspaper Collection, which is part of the British Library. After the passing of the Stamp Act in 1712, a copy of every published paper had to be deposited with the Inland Revenue. Many were subsequently destroyed, but the remainder were transferred in 1823 to the British Museum (now the British Library), which since then has housed a vast and ever-growing collection of British national, regional and local newspapers. Items before 1827 have been acquired by the purchase of private libraries, the most important being the Thomason and Burney Collections, which are kept at the main library in Great Russell St, London, WC1B 3DG.

The 'Thomason Tracts' include over 7,000 news-sheets from the period 1641-60. These are entered alphabetically in the library's General Index, and in addition are catalogued separately in chronological order. The Burney Collection (now microfilmed in title order) includes hundreds of volumes of British newspapers (including Scottish and Irish), again housed in the main library. These too are listed in the library's index. Dr Burney's own manuscript list is also available at the Enquiry Desk.

Most of the British Library's collection, however, is housed in its special British Newspaper Library at Colindale in North London. Nationally, this is the largest single collection of newspapers, with 500,000 volumes and 90,000 reels of microfilm. Here will be found the *Catalogue of the Newspaper Library* (1975), in eight volumes. This is the indispensable reference

1855.

KENT CATTLE and POULTRY SHOW.

FIFTEENTH EXHIBITION, in the COLLEGE YARD, MAIDSTONE, TUESDAY, DECEMBER 11th, for Horses, Cattle, Sheep, Pigs, Wool, Roots, and Poultry.

Open from Eight o'clock in the morning till Three o'clock in the afternoon. Admission 1s.

Horses, Cattle, Sheep, Pigs, Wool, Roots, or Poultry, will not be entitled to a premium unless brought to the place of exhibition before Ten o'clock on Monday, December 10th.

The place of exhibition will be open for their reception on Saturday previous to the Show Day, between the hours of 7 in the morning and 5 in the evening; and it is particularly requested that Exhibitors residing in the neighbourhood will not send their Poultry previous to Monday, 10th December.

A DINNER will be provided at the MitreHotel, on Tuesday, the 11th.

The Right Hon. LORD DE LISLE and DUDLEY, in the chair.

Tickets, 10s each, including a bottle of wine, to be had at the bar of the Hotel, where a plan of the room may be seen.

N.B.—As every seat in the room will be numbered, it is particularly requested that gentlemen intending to dine will make an early application for Tickets.

EDWARD RUSSELL TANNER,
Hon. Sec.

FEMALE EDUCATION.—FAMILIES
desirous of placing their Daughters in a first-class School, in the neighbourhood of London, may obtain Prospectuses of an Establishment of the highest character by applying to Mr. J. S. ISAAC, High-street, Maidstone.

References of the most satisfactory character can be given.

ROYAL STAR HOTEL, HIGH STREET,
MAIDSTONE.—MR. W. R. PINE, having taken that old-established house, the ROYAL STAR HOTEL, begs to inform the nobility, gentry, and inhabitants of Maidstone, and the neighbourhood, that he has made considerable alterations and improvements, and trusts, by strict attention to the wishes of those who may honour him with their patronage, to maintain the high character for the excellence of its accommodation which this celebrated Hotel has so long enjoyed.

Private families will find this an agreeable temporary residence.

TO OUR SUBSCRIBERS.

In consequence of the New Act respecting the Stamping of Newspapers, the price of this Journal will, on and after this day, be 5d. stamped, and 4d. unstamped.

A *stamped* copy can be sent by post, free, as often as may be desired, during fifteen days from the date of the paper, the folding being such as to show the stamp distinctly outside. *Unstamped* copies cannot be transmitted without affixing a penny postage-stamp every time it is sent through the post-office.

Stamped copies may be sent to the British colonies, the *South Eastern Gazette* having been registered for transmission beyond the United Kingdom. Unstamped papers can only be sent at the same postage rates as letters.

South Eastern Gazette.

MAIDSTONE and BIDDENDEN ROADS.

NOTICE IS HEREBY GIVEN, that the Tolls payable at the several Toll Gates upon the Turnpike Roads leading from Biddenden and Smarden to Maidstone, called "Franks Bridge Gate," "Thorpe's Gate," "Sutton Gate," and "Otham Gate," will be separately

LET BY AUCTION,

at the GEORGE INN, HEADCORN, on WEDNESDAY, the 12th day of DECEMBER next, to the best bidders, between the hours of 11 and 3, in the manner directed by the Act passed in the third year of the Reign of his late Majesty King George the Third, for One Year, from the 31st day of December next; which Tolls were let last year at the following sums:—

	£
Otham Gate and Sutton Gate, with Side-bar at Sutton	290
Thorpe's Gate	147
Franks Bridge Gate	220
Contract with Carriers	30

Whoever happen to be the best bidders must, at the same time, pay in advance the amount of One Month's Rent, and give Security, with sufficient Sureties, to the satisfaction of the Trustees for payment of the remainder by monthly instalments.

WILDES AND SON,
Clerks to the Trustees.

Maidstone, 12th Nov., 1855.

KENT GENERAL SESSION.

THE ANNUAL GENERAL SESSION, Under an Act passed in the year 1814, for enabling the Justices of the Peace for the County of Kent to hold a General Session annually, or oftener, for levying and applying the Rates and Expenditure of the said County, and to alter and amend an Act passed in the Forty-ninth year of his late Majesty King George the Third, for regulating the Rates of the said County, will be holden (by adjournment) at the COURT HOUSE, at MAIDSTONE,

On MONDAY, the 10th day of DECEMBER next,

At half-past 12 o'clock in the afternoon precisely, on business relating to the Assessment, Application, and Management of the County Stock or Rate, and on other business of the Annual General Session.

And NOTICE is Hereby Given, that it is intended at such Session to take into consideration the subject of building, providing, enlarging, and improving Lock-up Houses for temporary confinement under the provisions of the Acts for the appointment and payment of Parish Constables in any of the several Divisions of the said County, and to make Orders relative thereto; and that such business will commence at 1 o'clock.

And NOTICE is hereby also given, that at such Session an application will be made under an Act passed in the twelfth year of the reign of her present Majesty, intituled "An Act for the holding of Petty Sessions of the Peace in Boroughs, and for providing places for the holding of such Petty Sessions in Counties and Boroughs," for a fit and proper place to be hired or otherwise provided for the holding of Petty Sessions of the Peace at Sandwich, within the Wingham Division of Saint Augustine, and that the expenses thereof and attendant thereon be paid out of the County Rate.

H. A. WILDES.
Clerk of the Peace for Kent.

Maidstone, 22nd November, 1855.

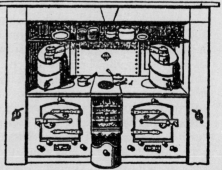

guide for those seriously interested in researching British local newspapers. (This catalogue is also available in some major reference and county libraries such as Birmingham.) Volume 1 deals mainly with London local newspapers, Volume 2 with the British Isles, and Volumes 3-4 with newspapers from overseas. The catalogue was completed in 1975, so it is more up to date than the *Times Tercentenary Handlist* published in 1920. However it is worth pointing out that, with early newspapers in particular, local libraries occasionally have more detailed and comprehensive holdings than the British Library, which concentrates mainly on 19th-century and later papers.

Before visiting Colindale (or any local repository), it is essential to check first that their holdings cover the period required and then, where possible, to book the use of a microfilm reader. The Newspaper Library is at Colindale Avenue, London NW6 5HE (Tel: 071-323-7353), opposite Colindale Underground Station on the Northern Line. It can also be reached from the Edgware Road just north of its intersection with the North Circular Road. The library is open six days a week (Mon.-Sat.) from 10 a.m. to 5 p.m., except on Bank Holidays and for an annual holiday which is normally the week following the last complete week in October. A reader's pass is required and may be obtained by writing to, or telephoning, the Superintendent. It may also be collected in person at Colindale or at the main British Library at Great Russell St. The Newspaper Library has a very small car park, but parking in nearby streets is unrestricted and relatively easy.

The best source for periodicals in the London area, for the 18th and early 19th centuries, is the *Old Bailey Sessions Papers*, sometimes referred to as the 'London Sessions Papers'. They were published immediately after the end of each session. A file of them can be found at the Guildhall Library.

The Bodleian Library at Oxford has a large collection of early newspapers. It is especially good for London newspapers in the period 1662-1732. All items are listed in the *Catalogue of English Newspapers and Periodicals in the Bodleian Library, 1662-1800* by R. T. Mitford and D. M. Sutherland (1936).

Finally the National Library of Wales at Aberystwyth (Tel: 0970 3816) holds the main collection of Welsh newspapers, while the National Library of Scotland in Edinburgh (Tel: 031-226-4531) houses the main Scottish collection. Titles of these newspapers are listed alphabetically, with an extra list under the names of towns and cities. A useful aid is *The Directory of Scottish Newspapers*, compiled by Joan P. F. Ferguson (1984), and published by the National Library.

INDEXING AND EXTRACTING

The value of old newspapers is now well recognised, but it can still be a daunting task to face a massive stack of files or microfilms without guidance. Until recently one of the greatest obstacles has been the lack of indexes analysing the contents of newspapers. Without such an index the task of searching can be laborious and protracted — which explains why most historians, both local and national, have therefore tended to use newspapers selectively or on a 'lucky dip' basis. The recent 'discovery' of newspapers as an important historical source has, however, encouraged libraries to tackle the enormous task of indexing. The fact is that the news content of papers can sometimes be easy and sometimes extremely difficult to exploit. Tasks or projects centring on a known date present few problems, for example the opening of a bridge, the closure of a tramway company, or a local election. One can turn to the appropriate newspaper for the relevant information and to later papers for reflections, comments and sometimes illustrations. However, to gain quick access to all the possible information contained in newspapers demands some form of indexing.

The idea of indexing is of course not new. Palmer's index to *The Times* is well known, and there are others such as the annual index to the *Glasgow Herald* (1906-68). Even so, a survey in 1981 discovered that indexes existed for only 114 titles. Since then, however, the situation has been radically transformed as a result of new initiatives, and by 1986 more than 650 indexes to local newspapers in Britain were available or had been started.

For example, in 1982 volunteers in Suffolk began to index the *Ipswich Journal* from the year 1800. Multiple entries are used; names, places and subjects including trades and professions. Lincolnshire, Cheshire, Cambridgeshire, Shropshire, Nottinghamshire and Gloucestershire have also got schemes in progress. Lincolnshire's project covers 15 titles published in six towns. Nottinghamshire's scheme involves seven titles. In Gloucestershire two indexes to the *Gloucester Journal* have been compiled. Many indexes begin with either the first issue or the first number of a library's holding. In the case of smaller towns, their newspapers often began shortly after the repeal of the Stamp Act in 1855, but many provincial cities had newspapers more than a century before. One such city, Liverpool, has indexed the l8th-century issues of Williamson's *Liverpool Advertiser*, whereas, for example, the indexes to the *Ipswich Journal* and *Nottingham Journal* do not begin until 1800.[14] Chester has published its newspaper index in book form. Any groups wanting to set up their own indexing project might very usefully consult this publication to see how the job can be done.

The Cambridgeshire Collection has a highly organised indexing project which is remarkably comprehensive and also commercial. Everything within the library system — newspapers, books, maps, pictures and tapes — are indexed cover to cover, paragraph to paragraph. For the period 1916-34 all pictures from newspapers are indexed, and from 1958 a cuttings file has also been available. The headings used match the catalogue numbers for books, and the cards themselves carry all the information needed by the researcher to find the material he or she wants, be it in a newspaper, in a book or elsewhere. A number of local groups in the county have also produced 'village chronicles' which detail local news and events in their respective parishes. In this way they are offering historians, whatever their detailed interests, the opportunity of drawing on the everyday life of many different communities. In addition they are providing invaluable raw material for writing the histories of individual parishes and towns, now and in the future.[15] Some would argue that this is the best use of local newspapers because it encourages a synoptic or 'total' approach to the past, in which local themes fruitfully overlap and merge. For example, a rural vicar who was genuinely concerned with the relief of the poor may be found to have opposed the setting up of a local school board; or a local historian may argue that the depressed state of the brick industry in the 1920s has some connection with chronic housing shortages in the inter-war years. Thus a parish history, fully referenced, can in some small measure act as an index.

7. Notice of a meeting to appoint a Collector of Poor Rates for an individual parish: *South Eastern Gazette*, 3 July 1855, p.1.

MEDWAY UNION.

A COLLECTOR of the POOR RATES for the parish of St. Margaret, in this Union.

The Guardians will, at their meeting, to be held at the Board Room, Chatham Workhouse, on *Wednesday*, the 11th of *July*, at Eleven o'clock in the forenoon, appoint a COLLECTOR of the POOR RATES for the parish of St. Margaret, in the place of Mr. C. Dorrett, who has resigned. The duties to be as prescribed by the orders of the Poor Law Board now in force, and the appointment and salary to be subject to their approval.

Further particulars may be known by applying at the Chatham Workhouse.

By order of the Board,
FRIEND HOAR, Clerk.

Board Room, July 2nd, 1855.

The index then can be extremely valuable for speedy access to information, and for finding dates. It is less useful, of course, for the historian not interested in single events but in the fluctuating life of the local community week by week, year by year. Subjects such as the movement of agricultural prices, the work of local firms, the development of local railway companies, and the regular meetings of magistrates and poor-law guardians have to be studied systematically over a period of time. Newspapers may also operate as a secondary source, publishing articles by antiquarians and local historians which might not otherwise be printed. Such pieces may often be reports of public lectures or details of surveys. In Wiltshire, for example, Edward Kite, historian of Devizes, published 40

8. Title of a local newspaper in the late 19th century; notice the price of one penny: *Herne Bay Argus,* 23 January 1892.

historical articles, including a series on old houses, in the *Devizes Gazette* between 1917 and 1929. Kite's reason for using a newspaper resulted from a quarrel with the Wiltshire Archaeological Society and from the demise in 1916 of the alternative periodical *Wiltshire Notes and Queries*.[16]

As mentioned above, some local libraries also possess files of 'cuttings' from newspapers. In certain instances they have been maintained since the last century. Such files can be extremely useful, especially if they are indexed. Any kind of subject could be covered. In addition cuttings may have attached to them photographs, programmes and other ephemera. It is always possible that such files include material from newspapers and periodicals no longer in existence. Enfield, for example, has many cuttings from *Paul Pry*, an early 19th-century newspaper which dealt largely in scandal. From the local historian's point of view, a good index is always preferable to a file of cuttings because of the problem of selective bias on the part of the librarian or researcher. The bias already inherent in a newspaper is compounded when a cutter decides what to preserve and what to reject. An item which may have seemed of no historical value at the time may be of major significance a century or so later, and vice versa.

Cuttings do, however, have some advantages. They may be grouped or filed in a systematic order based on a classification scheme. They may be easily photocopied. Where extensive cuttings are available for local historians, they are usually well used. Belfast claims that its series of 88 fully indexed books of cuttings dating from 1900 is possibly the single most used source in the Irish Studies Collection. Gloucester has 30 volumes of cuttings which begin in 1859, and is now indexing them on cards. Clwyd, on the other hand, stores its collection on microfiche.

In 1972 W. G. Hoskins offered an index of master headings compiled after much thought by a local history group in the University of Hull.[17] These are an attempt to cover all the possible topics that a local historian could reasonably expect to get from a newspaper of the early 19th century. Each of the main headings selected could of course have a number of subsidiary headings, for example:

An expanded version of the master headings is reprinted in Appendix 1 (p. 23) as an aid to those who are thinking of indexing local newspapers.

9. Advertisements from the *South Eastern Gazette*, 3 July 1855, p.1.

FURTHER PROBLEMS

It is clear then that newspapers must be regarded as very important documents for local historical purposes. Newspaper archives and local history collections in reference libraries or county record offices can be fascinating hunting grounds for local historians. Although they are printed, newspapers are in every sense primary sources and should be treated in the same way as one deals, for example, with tithe apportionments or probate records. Excellent as they are, a big disincentive to making full and extensive use of newspapers is their bulk. The result is that they have been primarily used in a subsidiary, selective fashion. There exist, as a result, many collections of reprinted extracts on particular themes, for example, *The Observer of the Nineteenth Century*, edited by M. Miliband (1966), or *Newspapers of The First World War*, edited by I. Williams (1970). Yet there is no substitute for conducting research in the files of newspapers themselves, or on the microfilmed versions which have been produced to preserve the fragile originals.

There is no denying that microfilm can be wearying to read for long periods, even on machines with large screens. Matters are not helped by the frequent smallness and closeness of the type, or by the absence of headlines or subheadings in the earlier prints. Another hazard is that the items which originally made newspapers interesting and saleable can often prove an embarrassing distraction to the researcher. Most local historians find it difficult to pursue a particular topic single-mindedly through the files, and to ignore everything else. This is why research on newspapers frequently takes far longer than one originally anticipated, and why many of us end up with many more notes and references than the original purpose demanded. This frequently includes references noted down for the benefit of one's friends and colleagues!

Another major problem is to decide whether or not to sample newspapers. It is true that random searches and quick samples based on the known dates of happenings can produce new and very exciting evidence. Similarly one may find useful material by sampling particular dates or seasons each year. But for any sustained piece of research in which newspapers are primary evidence, we really have no alternative to working fully and relentlessly through the files, one by one, for the period concerned. This is certainly time-consuming and underlines the importance of choosing a subject which is viable and not too large in terms of the work involved. Sometimes, in the light of experience, it simply becomes necessary to redefine the topic to make it more manageable. Generally, therefore, sampling from each yearly volume causes us to miss important items, and introduces the possibility that our evidence is over-simplified and thereby less complete than it need be.

Living in the later 20th century, we can have little doubt that newspaper reporting, news and comment can be a distortion of reality. Information is changed, reorganised and selected by journalists, editors and owners. As G. K. Chesterton in one of his essays reminded us, 'Life is one world, and life seen in the newspapers is another'.[18] The historian using the press must have a good grasp of contemporary history, must know what to accept and what to question, and be prepared to dig for the truth. This is not an easy process, for what newspapers do not report is often as relevant as what they do.

How reliable, then, are local newspapers? Clearly they are an intentional record, and therefore searching questions must be asked. How and why did the newspaper come into existence? Who founded it and for what purpose? What are the political and other beliefs of owners or editors? What is the historical context of the news? Are there other sources or rival newspapers against which to check what a newspaper says? In Chesterfield, for example, *The Derbyshire Times* firmly supported the established political order in Church and State, but you have to read the *Derbyshire Courier* for reportage of Nonconformist activities. Either newspaper on its own gives a one-sided and therefore distorted picture of contemporary events. Some journals positively welcomed the establishment of a rival print. The *Northampton Journal* founded in 1772 was in some ways a godsend to the struggling *Mercury*, founded in 1770. Battle was immediately joined, insults were hurled and the resultant competition for readers considerably enlivened the pages of both newspapers. There was a similar outcome in Cambridge when Benjamin Flower's radical *Cambridge Intelligencer* clashed with Francis Hodson's *Chronicle* over the conduct of the Napoleonic War, the role of the church, and alleged political corruption in the town.

One of the key questions asked about newspapers is whether they influence or merely reflect public opinion. Writing in the early 19th century the editor of the *Sheffield Iris* had his answer: 'Newspapers are first what public opinion makes them; then by a curious reaction they make public opinion what they please . . .'.[19] Clearly the impact of the press was often indirect during this period, and many contemporaries were not aware of what was happening. Richard Cobden looking back over the first 50 years of the century argued that the editors of the great London and provincial prints, who had led public opinion, had played a part in the Industrial Revolution as important as that of the great inventors. Gladstone in 1892 said that 'the three Ps have denoted the instruments by which British Freedom has been principally developed and confirmed. These three Ps are Petition, Press and Platform'.[20] By the early 20th century newspapers were run by great 'press barons' and were no longer (if they ever were) politically free. The new goal was mass circulation, or as J. R. Scott of the *Manchester Guardian* had put it, 'to make readable righteousness remunerative'.[21]

In attempting to assess the power of the press, it should be borne in mind that editorials are expressions of an editor's views and do not guarantee the prevalence of those opinions. The selection of readers' letters for publication is, of course, also a matter for the editor. We have, moreover, Paul Addison's warning to the historian of public opinion: 'Judgements about the "movement" of popular opinion have always been tempered by the knowledge that many people never change their opinions, while some never have any to change'.[22] An alternative to concentrating on the development of editorial opinion is the technique of 'content analysis', a method taken from the social sciences and first used in the 1930s by opinion polls, market research and 'Mass Observation' surveys. The underlying assumption is that attitudes and reactions can be quantified and measured. As Victoria Berridge has shown in the case of the popular Victorian Sunday press, content analysis can be used to examine such issues as the influence of advertising and the concentration of press ownership. It may also be employed in studying the function of the newspaper within society.[23]

Other difficulties arise when we look beyond the content of newspapers. Circulation figures, which supply a clue of sorts to newspaper influence, are by no means as abundant

CIRCULATION OF THE KENTISH PAPERS.
GOVERNMENT RETURNS.

Official return of the Circulation of the Kentish Newspapers for the Three Years ending December, 1853; and for the year ending December, 1854.

	1851, '52, '53.	1854.	Weekly.
South Eastern Gazette	383,030	156,500 ..	3,010
Maidstone Journal	175,225	81,100 ..	1,559
Kentish Gazette	161,511	51,500 ..	990
Kent Herald	141,000	43,000 ..	827
Kentish Mercury...............	95,275	41,975 ..	807
Dover Chronicle	61,000	33,750 ..	648
Dover Telegraph	97,200	32,050 ..	616
Kentish Independent...........	67,000	22,000 ..	423
Kentish Observer..............	50,500	19,000 ..	367
Canterbury Journal	28,500	7,000 ..	135
Rochester Gazette....	21,000	4,000 ..	
West Kent Guardian	14,652	4,669 ..	
Woolwich Gazette	11,969	2,236 ..	

AS AN ADVERTISING MEDIUM

The value of the South Eastern Gazette may thus be clearly estimated. Its appreciation can be ascertained from the following comparison of numbers of advertisements, counted from the files of the Gazette and Maidstone Journal, the nexthighest in circulation:—

	1844.	'45.	'46.	'47.	'48.	'49.	'50.	'51.	'52.
Gazette	4,049	4,243	4,302	5,160	5,282	5,417	5,827	5,952	6,378
Journal	3,498	3,380	3,183	4,024	3,705	3,616	3,787	3,734	4,088

Excess	551	863	1,119	1,136	1,577	1,801	2,040	2,228	2,290

And during 1853 and 1854 this paper has obtained a still higher position, as may be seen by the following numbers:—

	1853.	1854.
South Eastern Gazette	8,552	11,213
Maidstone Journal	4,693	6,146
Kentish Gazette	3,499	4,097

Thus showing the South Eastern Gazette to have a larger number of advertisements than both of the next highest papers in the county together.

10. Table showing circulation figures for newspapers in Kent: *South Eastern Gazette*, 3 July 1855, p.4.

as we would wish; and those which exist are not necessarily reliable. Indeed, the only fully documented period is that between the reduction of the stamp duty in 1836 and its abolition in 1855. For a comprehensive discussion of this issue the researcher is referred to a paper by A. P. Wadsworth, a former editor of the *Manchester Guardian*, entitled 'Newspaper circulation, 1800-1954' and published in *Transactions of the Manchester Statistical Society* (1954-5). Moreover, with some notable exceptions — for example, *The Times* and the *Manchester Guardian* — the press historian is frequently handicapped by the paucity of surviving office records. H. R. G. Whates quotes the proprietor of a prominent London newspaper: 'The *Daily Telegraph* may have broken records . . . certainly it kept none'. In writing the history of the *Birmingham Daily Post*, Whates himself had to rely upon 'casual references in books by members of the staff, a few scrappy memoranda and letters, a fairly reliable memory, and the files of the newspaper itself'.[24]

The processes behind the making of the newspaper remain elusive. R. K. Webb referred to the 'near impossibility of getting behind the anonymity of writing for the newspaper press'.[25] As Lucy Brown points out, authorship can sometimes be found in memoirs, but journalists can move rapidly between jobs and their memoirs carry no guarantee of accuracy.[26] As a general rule the workings of the press must be reconstructed from the printed newspaper files and from any other records which may chance to survive.

The most important aspect of newspapers to many people is their urgency and immediacy. They are a record of history as it is being made. Researching them gives us an insight into how the public received and reacted to news at the time. Provided that the newspaper is used critically and judiciously, its merits as an historical source greatly outweigh its shortcomings. The study of local newspapers may be a painstaking task, but no less worthwhile for that. In the dusty archives of the newspaper press are vast resources, still waiting to be tapped and exploited.

APPENDIX 1
(*see* p. 19)

Master headings suggested for indexing newspapers (after W. G. Hoskins, 1972)

Acts of Parliament
Agriculture
Amusements
Antiquities
Architecture
Army
Associations (miscellaneous)
Banks (and Finance)
Brewing and Inns
Bridges
Canals
Charities
Children
Class
Commerce
Costume
Crafts
Crime
Customs (local)
Education
Elections
Emigration
Enclosures
Erosion
Factories
Fairs
Families
Farming
Firms
Fishing
Food and Drink
Freemasonry
Furniture
Harbours
Horticulture
Hospitals
Improvements
Industries
Inns (*see* Brewing)
Inventions
Irrigation
Justice (*see* Police)
Land Use
Law and Order
Lawyers
Leisure
Libraries
Lighting
Literature

Living Conditions
Local Government
Markets
Medicine and Surgery
M.P.s
Mills
Museums
Music
Navigation
Navy
Newspapers
Parishes
Parliament
Personalities
Philanthropy
Police
Political Parties
Population
Postal Services
Poverty (and Poor Law)
Prices
Printing and Publishing
Professions
Property
Public Health
Publishing (*see* Printing)
Railways
Recipes
Religion
Riots
Roads
Shipping
Smuggling
Sport
Streets
Strikes
Theatre
Topography
Towns
Trade Unions
Transport
Travel
Villages
Wages
Wars
Waterways
Weather
Women
Workhouses

NOTES

1. M. J. Murphy, *Cambridge Newspapers and Opinion, 1750-1850* (Cambridge, 1977), p. 7.
2. John Westmancoat, *Newspapers* (London, 1985), p. 17.
3. J. Black, 'Newspapers and Politics in the 18th Century', *History Today* (Oct. 1986), p. 42.
4. For a general introduction to the early history of the Press, see G. A. Cranfield, *The Development of the Provincial Newspaper, 1700-1760* (Oxford, 1962) and his *The Press and Society: from Caxton to Northcliffe* (London, 1978); R. M. Wiles, *Freshest Advices, Early Provincial Newspapers in England* (1965).
5. See S. Koss, *The Rise and Fall of the Political Press in Britain* (Trowbridge, 1981).
6. G. Boyce, J. Curran & P. Wingate (eds), *Newspaper History from the 17th Century to the Present Day* (London, 1978), p. 131.
7. M. Milne, 'The Historian and Local Newspapers', *Local Studies Librarian*, I (1982), p. 6.
8. Quoted in T. Baistow, *Fourth-Rate Estate* (Old Woking, 1985), p. 1.
9. Black, 'Newspapers and Politics in the 18th Century', p. 36.
10. Cranfield, *Press and Society*, Ch. 7; Murphy, *Cambridge Newspapers*, Ch. 2; Milne, 'The Historian and Local Newspapers', p. 5; D. Read, *Press and People, 1790-1850* (London, 1961), pp. 69-70.
11. Quoted in Boyce *et al.*, *Newspaper History*, p. 107.
12. J. R. Ravensdale, *History on your Doorstep* (London, 1982), p. 142.
13. J. West, *Town Records* (Chichester, 1983), Ch. 6.
14. See K. A. MacMahon, 'Local History and the Newspaper', *The Amateur Historian*, V (1961-3); D. Iredale, *Enjoying Archives* (Chichester, 1985), Ch. 10; M. Dewe (ed.), *Local Studies Librarianship* (Aldershot, 1987), p. 234-9.
15. M. Petty, 'Cambridge Newspapers and the Local Researcher', Cambridgeshire Collection handout (1966).
16. Dewe (ed.), *Local Studies Librarianship*, p. 235.
17. W. G. Hoskins, *Local History in England* (London, 1972), pp. 213-15.
18. Quoted in E. Hildick, *A Close Look at Newspapers* (1966), p. 206.
19. Cranfield, *Press and Society*, p. 202.
20. Quoted in Murphy, *Cambridge Newspapers*, p. 8.
21. Quoted in Boyce *et al.*, *Newspaper History*, p. 128.
22. P. Addison, *The Road to 1945: British Politics and the Second World War* (London, 1977), p. 15.
23. V. Berridge, 'Content Analysis and Historical Research on Newspapers' in M. Harris & A. Lee (eds), *The Press in English Society from the 17th to the 19th Centuries* (London, 1986), p. 201-18.
24. H. R. G. Whates, *The Birmingham Post, 1857-1957* (Birmingham, 1957), p. 3.
25. R. K. Webb, *The British Working Class Reader* (London, 1955), p. vii.
26. L. Brown, *Victorian News and Newspapers* (Oxford, 1985), p. 3.